Christmas is Coming!
Advent Coloring Book

Mary Lou Brown & Sandy Mahony

December 1

December 2

December 3

December 4

December 5

December 6

December 7

December 8

December 9

December 10

December 11

December 12

December 13

December 14

December 15

December 16

December 17

December 18

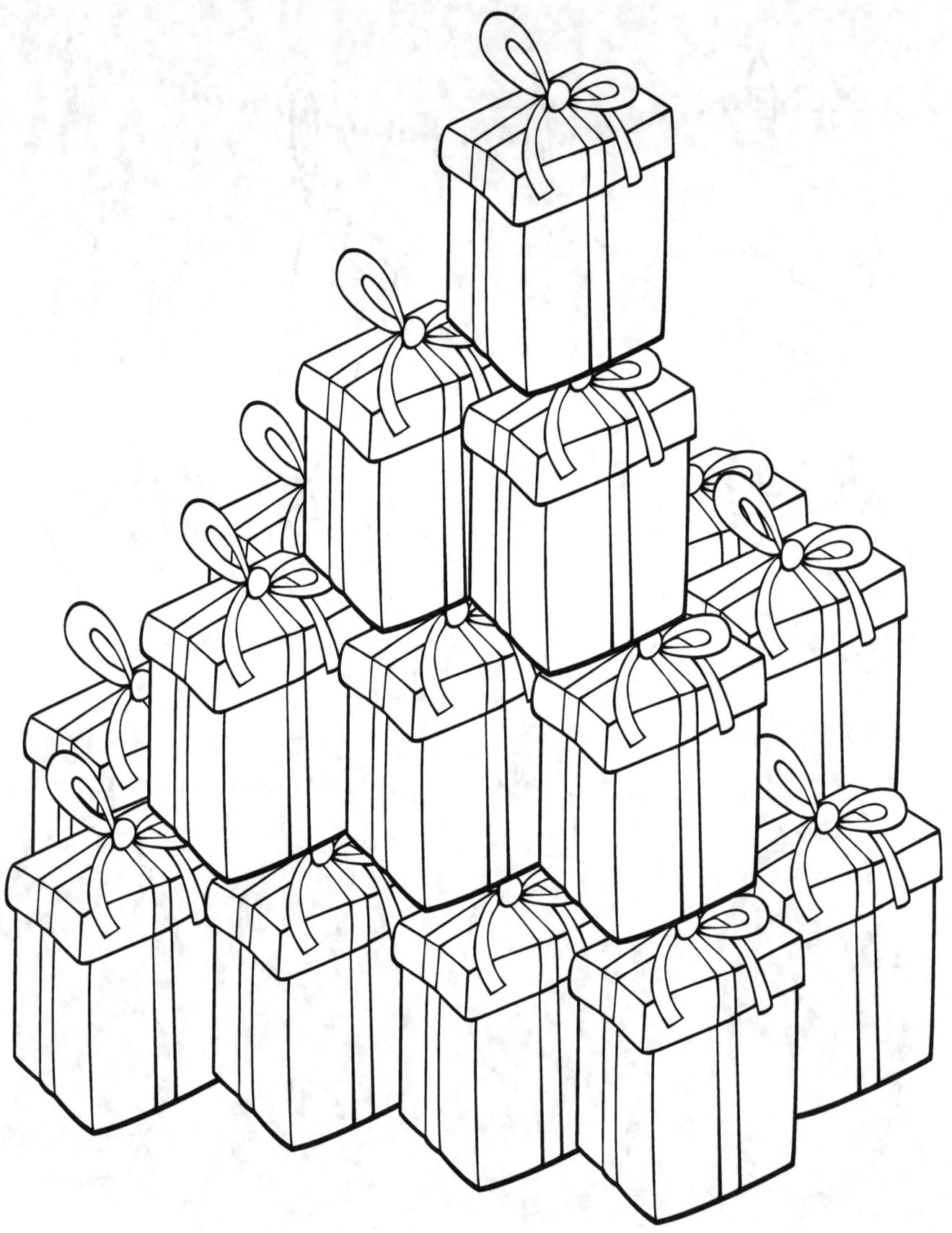

December 19

December 20

December 21

December 22

December 23

December 24

December 25

Merry Christmas

adventurelearningpress.com

www.ingramcontent.com/pod-product-compliance
Lightning Source LLC
Chambersburg PA
CBHW081810280526
45789CB00008B/3074